Contemplations on Fairy Tales

I

About the Four Skillful Brothers

by

Rudolf Geiger

Translated from the German
by Ruth Pusch

MERCURY PRESS

This translation was taken from *Märchenkunde: Mensch und Schicksal im Spiegel der Grimmschen Märchen*, Rudolf Geiger, Verlag Urachhaus, 1982. Permission was kindly granted by the author and publisher.

The fairy tale *The Four Skillful Brothers* from the Brothers Grimm has been taken chiefly from the translation of Margaret Hunt in the Pantheon edition of 1944.

Cover by Kitsie McHenry

ISBN 0-929979-11-7

Printed and published in the USA by
MERCURY PRESS
Fellowship Community
241 Hungry Hollow Road
Spring Valley, NY 10977

Fachinger, Petra. "A New Kind of Creative Energy: Yadé Kara's *Selam Berlin* and Fatih Akin's *Kurz und Schmerzlos* and *Gegen die Wand*." *German Life and Letters* 60.2 (April 2007): 243–60.

——. *Re-writing Germany from the Margins*. Montreal: McGill-Queen's UP, 2001.

Freud, Sigmund. *Civilization and its Discontents*. Ed. and Trans. James Strachey. New York: W. W. Norton & Company, 1989.

Gramling, David. "On the Other Side of Monolingualism: Fatih Akin's Linguistic Turn(s)." *The German Quarterly* 83.3 (Summer 2010): 353–72.

Halberstam, Jack. "Introduction." *The Undercommons: Fugitive Planning & Black Study*. New York: Minor Compositions, 2013. 2–12.

Hitchcock, Peter. *Dialogics of the Oppressed*. Minneapolis: U of Minnesota P, 1993.

Kim, John Namjun. "Ethnic Irony: The Poetic Parabasis of the Promiscuous Personal Pronoun in Yoko Tawada's 'Eine leere Flasche' (A Vacuous Flask)." *The German Quarterly* 83.3 (Summer 2010): 333–52.

Kristeva, Julia. "Word, Dialogue and Novel." Trans. Alice Jardine, Thomas Gora, and Leon S. Roudiez. *The Kristeva Reader*. Ed. Toril Moi. New York: Columbia UP, 1986. 34–61.

Marriott, David. *Haunted Life: Visual Culture and Black Modernity*. New Brunswick: Rutgers UP, 2007.

Moten, Fred. "Black Op." *PMLA* 123.5 (2008): 1743–7.

——. and Stefano Harney. *The Undercommons: Fugitive Planning & Black Study*. New York: Minor Compositions, 2013.

Sexton, Jared. "The Social Life of Social Death." *InTensions Journal* 5 (Fall/Winter 2011). York University. Web.

Silva, Denise Ferreira da. *Toward a Global Idea of Race*. Minneapolis: U of Minnesota P, 2005.

Spivak, Gayatri Chakravorty. "Can the Subaltern Speak?" *Marxism and the Interpretation of Culture*. Ed. C. Nelson and L. Grossberg. Basingstoke: Macmillan Education, 1998. 271–313.

Veteto-Conrad, Marilya. "'Innere Unruhe'? Zehra Çirak and Minority Literature Today." *Rocky Mountain Review of Language and Literature* 53.2 (1999): 59–74.

——. "Zehra Çirak: Foreign Wings on Familiar Shoulders." *Homemaking: Women Writers and the Politics and Poetics of Home*. Ed. Catherine Wiley and Fiona R. Barnes. New York: Garland Publishing, 1996. 335–59.

Wilderson, Frank B. III. "The Vengeance of Vertigo: Aphasia and Abjection in the Political Trials of Black Insurgents." *InTensions Journal* 5 (Fall/Winter 2011). York University. Web.

William, Jennifer Marston. "Cognitive Poetics and Common Ground in a Multicultural Context: The Poetry of Zehra Çirak." *The German Quarterly* 85.2 (Spring 2012): 173–92.

Winnicott, D. W. "The Concept of a Healthy Individual." *Home is Where We Start From: Essays by a Psychoanalyst*. New York: W. W. Norton & Company, 1990. 21–34.

——. *Playing and Reality*. London: Routledge, 2005.

——. "Primitive Emotional Development." *Collected Papers: Through Paediatrics to Psycho-Analysis*. New York: Basic Books, 1958. 145–56.

matter of the apprehension of psychic—and political—reality in a properly psychoanalytic sense: an effect of misrecognition, a problem of register and symbolization, an optical illusion or echo that dissimulates the course and force of its propagation" (36). Sexton describes how the affective response of "anxiety" or "aggression" registers psychic and political reality, the reality of misrecognition, the effect of being misrecognized that attends a subject who is thought through the scheme of dependency that constantly references identity's negativity.

10. See Jennifer Marston William's reading of the metaphors invoked in this title in "Cognitive Poetics and Common Ground in a Multicultural Context: The Poetry of Zehra Çirak" (184).

11. Marilya Veteto-Conrad translates this title "No Sand in the Gears of Time" in "Zehra Çirak: Foreign Wings on Familiar Shoulders" (356–7).

12. Fred Moten uses the formulation "not but nothing other than," which I find logically appealing as a formula for poetic dialogism, to phrase the relationship between blackness and Western civilization: "Blackness is not but nothing other than Western civilization" (1744).

13. This quotation is a summary by *profacero* of Silva's *Toward a Global Idea of Race* posted under the entry "Breakdown of Denise Ferreira da Silva: *Toward a Global Theory of Race*" (12 March 2009) on the blog *Seminario Permanente de Teoria y Critica*.

14. Like Çirak, Sexton seems to find that the "world" exists as a desire, as a desire for integration: "No, Blackness is not the pathogen in afro-pessimism, the world is. Not the earth, but the world, and maybe even the whole possibility of and desire for a world" (30).

Works cited

Adelson, Leslie. *The Turkish Turn in Contemporary German Literature*. London: Palgrave Macmillan, 2005.

Adorno, Theodor. "On Lyric Poetry and Society." *Notes to Literature I*. Trans. Shierry Weber Nicholson. New York: Columbia UP, 1991. 37–54.

Bakhtin, Mikhail. "Discourse in the Novel." *The Dialogic Imagination: Four Essays by M.M. Bakhtin*. Ed. Michael Holquist. Trans. Caryl Emerson and Michael Holquist. Austin: U of Texas P, 1981. 259–422.

Balibar, Etienne. "Europe as Borderland." Talk given for the Alexander von Humboldt Lecture in Human Geography, University of Nijmegen, November 10, 2004.

——. "The Geneological Scheme: Race or Culture." *Trans-Scripts* 1 (2011): 1–9.

——. *We, the People of Europe? Reflections on Transnational Citizenship*. Trans. James Swenson. Princeton: Princeton UP, 2004.

Çirak, Zehra. *Fremde Flügel auf Eigener Schulter*. Cologne: Kiepenheuer & Witsch, 1994.

——. *Vogel auf dem Rücken eines Elefanten*. Cologne: Kiepenheuer & Witsch, 1991.

De Man, Paul. "Dialogism and Dialogue." *Resistance to Theory*. Minneapolis: U of Minnesota P, 1986. 106–14.

——. "The Epistemology of Metaphor." *Critical Inquiry* 5.1 (Autumn 1978): 13–30.

Enzensberger, Hans Magnus. "Poetry and Politics." Trans. Michael Roloff. *Critical Essays*. Ed. Reinhold Grimm. New York: Continuum, 1982. 15–34.

Introduction

Thirty years ago Rudolf Geiger began to tell fairy tales to groups of children, including his own—accompanied by a series of pictures he had made of many-layered, many-colored tissue paper, lit up in magic lantern style. Soon more and more adults joined this fairy tale activity; they found they had not grown away from the wonders that strike such a deep melody in us. Geiger continued to tell the tales but gradually gave up the bright pictures, when he realized that, because today our imaginations are so overloaded from outside, we are hungry for the fairy tale imaginations that can rise up within ourselves in the vivid and restorative way they did in past ages.

Rudolf Geiger came to his devotion to the tales through his colleague in Freiburg, Germany: Dr. Friedrich Husemann, a doctor who specialized in soul illnesses and who had found that fairy tales are strong and heartening medicine. He and then Rudolf Geiger had special sessions just for adults, bringing one or the other tale, long lived with, to a kind of imaginative contemplation.

We hope to bring out further "contemplations" on the Grimms' tales. Geiger published over forty in his book *Märchenkunde* and is loath to call them explanatory. It was George Macdonald, wonderful creator of his own wonder-stories, who said, "Fairy tales do not convey a meaning; they *awake* a meaning." Each person, in experiencing the light-filled warmth of the tales, will—and should—find his own interpretation. That is the purpose of this booklet, which is, of course, only for adult consideration. But if it can encourage each reader to spend time with these and other fairy tales and actually *tell* the tales to a child or children at hand (who are

1

waiting hungrily for such a blessing)—without a book or machine standing in between mouth and ear, one could say between soul and soul—this book will have begun a joyful opening up of treasure.

Ruth Pusch
Spring Valley, 1990

The Four Skillful Brothers

I

As in so many fairy tales, the beginning of this tale is poverty. Of course, if there were no poverty, nothing would happen that has to happen. The scene opens in the middle of a bare time; the riches of an earlier era have been used up.

There was once a poor man who had four sons, and when they were grown up, he said to them, 'Dear children, you must now go out into the world, for I have nothing to give you. Set out and learn a trade and see how you can make your way.

The father may well have been sorry for his blunt decree but it wouldn't help things. The next generation has to do better, come what may. His sons must progress by their own efforts. "Learn a trade and see how you get on." The father—opening his door—is urging each son to *become himself*, out there in the world, in the misery of exile.

So the four brothers took up their wander-staffs, said farewell to their father and went through the gate together.

The tale doesn't tell us whether they were given food for the journey; it was probably little enough anyway. But each of the four took up his "wander-staff". That is their father's order, which holds them upright, first as a stick to support them, later a part of their character when each can stand on his own feet without outer support. The wander-staff is their only inheritance—can they transform it into a sceptre?

When they had travelled some little distance, they came to a crossroads, which branched off in four different directions. Then said the eldest, "Here we must separate, but at this

3

*spot four years hence we will meet each other again and in
the meantime seek our fortunes." So each went his way.*

Up to the crossroads they stay together, united, brothers of
one family, without distinction. "Dear children," the father
has said—and that is what they have been to this point, mere
children. But at the crossroads their individualities begin to
appear, first of all as to age. We hear the eldest speak, with
thoughtful words. In a moment the second, third, and finally
the youngest will be identified.

At the crossroads, the four are presented as individuals.
We might have expected them to proceed two by two, but
only much later, at the end of the story, will they find their
own twin.

The crossroads separates them; each one goes his own
way. The brotherhood is split apart. What was an enclosing
circle in the father's house, a world of security, has broken at
the crossroads into the earthly paths of destiny that each person has to discover for himself. The cross is the symbol of be-
coming an individual.

Let us think for a moment of this sign. A vertical descends
downward, coming from above and seeking its roots below.
Another stream, in contrast, comes from the far side and
moves into the distance on the other side, vanishing away at
the horizon, crossing the stability of the vertical as purest con-
tradiction. In the cross the two directions pierce each other in
opposition. But once they find the exact right angle to each
other, they unite in a new way: out of the mere "crossing" a
unique harmony creates firmness. All the work of the weaver,
for instance, rests on this law of the crossing. From the warp
stretched vertically and the woof horizontally by the weaver's
hands, the woven cloth grows into an earthly garment. And

4

we are all weaving our life's tapestry in this way, from standing to withstanding, from being stretched to thrusting the shuttle.

The cross is symbol of the earth. The Spirit of the Sun who willed to unite with the earth had to bind Himself to the cross, in order to enter fully into this sphere. That is the reason why the Christ, of all spiritual beings, wears the sign of the cross within the cosmic circle of His Sun-aura; thus He is distinguished from the other sublime beings as the overruling Spirit of the Earth.

Keep this in mind: at the crossroads the brothers set out towards their individual destinies; they agree to separate and are ready for what is to come. Until that moment there were certainly inherent differences and now they will be obliged to develop them. The oldest brother speaks it out: "Here we must separate... and seek our fortunes." Every individual path conceals an adventure! Not one of the brothers knows what is ahead, yet they promise to find their way back together, for, after all, they are children of *one* father, to whom they will return. And so their time-journey begins into the unknown. They leave each other, each one thinking only of himself at the moment; for four years each one will forget the others.

II

It is astonishing how differently, when they separate, the four sons develop their capacities. What diversity unfolds! Just listen:

The eldest met a man who asked him where he was going and what he intended to do. "I want to learn a trade," he replied. "Oh", said the man, "come with me and learn to be

5

a thief." "No," replied the youth, "that is not a reputable trade and at the end of it one has to swing on the gallows." "Ha," replied the man, "you need not be afraid of the gallows. I will teach you only to get such things as no other man could ever lay hold of, and so cleverly that others will never find it out." So he allowed himself to be talked into it and became, while with the man, so skillful in sleight of hand that nothing was safe from him if he once desired to have it.

The second brother met a man who put the same question to him—what he would like to learn in the world.

"I don't know yet," he replied. "Then come with me and become a star-gazer," said the man. "There is nothing better than that, for nothing can be hidden from you." The second brother liked the idea and became such a skillful astronomer that when he had learned everything and was about to travel onwards, his master gave him a telescope, saying, "With this you can see whatever is going on, both on earth and in heaven; nothing can be hidden from you."

A huntsman took the third brother as his apprentice and taught him everything that a clever hunter should know, so that very few huntsmen could equal him. When he went away, his master presented him with a gun and said, "Whatever you aim at with this you will not fail to hit."

The youngest brother also met with a man who spoke to him and asked him what his intentions were. "Would you not like to be a tailor?"

"I think not," replied the youth. "Sitting doubled up from morning to night driving the needle and iron constantly back and forth would not suit me at all."

"Oh, but you are talking of what you do not understand," replied the man. "With me you would learn a very different

6

art of tailoring which is far more respectable and seemly and for the most part, very honorable."

So he let himself be persuaded, went with the man and learned his art from the ground up. When they parted, his master gave him a needle, saying. "With this you can sew together whatever comes your way, whether it is soft as an egg or hard as steel: and it will join it together like one piece of stuff so that no seam is visible."

For all sorts of reasons you should have the original phrasing in order to understand how deep and many-layered the description is. The professions/crafts appear at first glance like the ordinary ones, and the eldest brother as well as the youngest brother at first do not relish what is offered them. But the conversation with the masters changes the grey, everyday view into what scintillates behind it, a profession behind the profession, an art behind the craft—until it seems as though it actually entails a supreme art. Each of the masters refers to the highest perfection of his art. We will come back to this later, as well as to the question, was it chance that led each brother to his master, the eldest to the master thief, the second to the star-gazer, the third to the huntsman and particularly the youngest to the tailor, who had a hard time winning over his apprentice?

If we look at the four professions, we can bring them into a relationship with each other and can try to establish their character. We can begin with the handiwork of the youngest brother, for it is his and the hunter's work that fit this word best; tailoring and hunting provide sturdy livelihoods and are "normal" professions. But star-gazer?—it has a queer sound, something of whims and crotchets, with dabbling in idleness, frittering away one's time. When you use the modern term, astronomer, however, the profession grows more respectable—but also grows up out of the everyday kind of work, takes on distance, becomes unattainable. The stargazer surely doesn't learn a "handcraft" and he couldn't join a guild or union. Similarly no one could imagine the thief as member of any honorable professional group. But let us forget the moralistic assessment and look at the activity of each profession. Here the professions take on unique relationships and contradictions—and these are the important elements of the tale.

Tailor and huntsman work by day, they require light to do their jobs. Their activity lies open and aboveboard. The hunter could even be described as appearing by choice in the early morning when nature is waking up and fresh (at noon it seems to fall asleep again). On the other hand, the tailor needs the full sunlight for his tiny, careful stitches; otherwise his eyes will smart. He works at the brightest window of his shop.

In contrast, the star-gazer and thief practice their arts at night. For them there should be concealing darkness, a time dismal, even sinister, to day-people. In the early evening the stargazer begins to be active and works late into the night. The thief prefers the time between midnight and dawn for his expeditions, for then most people are sound asleep. And so we see that we can put our four brothers into the four parts of the day that suit them best; early morning the huntsman, high noon the tailor, evening the stargazer, past midnight the thief.

Tailor and huntsman, the day people, are dissimilar in their working area; the tailor is always at home, keeps to his room and spends his life sitting down with his legs under him. This bodily position is just what the youngest brother had objected to. On the other hand, the huntsman's space widens out over fields and forest, for he loves ranging far and wide. His life is utmost movement, his feet are as important as the tailor's hands. Neither one could exchange his spatial needs with the other.

The contrast tailor/huntsman can go as far as their bodily form. In all our fairy tales the tailor is small and frail, a little man dried up from living alone in his shop. The huntsman, we imagine as big and muscular, an athlete, open and friendly in his gestures; he lives with natural things and is the original nature-boy. His senses are alert and take in the whole landscape. The tailor, small and clever, knows how to measure, is quick at figuring and can manage things to his own advantage. Though he's frail, he likes to boast about his courage. If he gets into the middle of a fight, however, he scrams and lets the giants' blows fall on each other, as in the tale of "The Brave Little Tailor." The huntsman, well used to hardships, goes after things fearlessly: he is usually a daredevil. He can stalk and track and find the wild game in the wild forests—even the savages there.

It's harder to characterize the star-gazer and the thief. There is something uncanny, even magic in the secret doings of a star-gazer. You can't tell what he's looking for or what he'll do with it. Ancient dusty pictures show him long and skinny, wearing the tall head-covering of a wizard. Elsewhere he's more like the Spitzweg portrait: the comfortably round, phlegmatic hermit—after all, a stargazer never does much more than look, observe, follow a sequence of happenings, avoid hurricanes and glare. His hands rest delicately on the instruments, while he sets them aright and reads the notation. He never is pulled into coarse matter; he lives alone, observing and pondering.

Still, one can say that the star-gazer is a reversed huntsman, who also lives by his eye, though his feet have to carry him to the place his eye wants to observe. Stalking game and scouring the landscape is what he loves to do. The star-gazer stays quietly in his tower; it's his eyes and thought that scour his field, the heavens. Both huntsman and star-gazer are discoverers. They follow the tracks of their game, each in his own way, each in quite a different way.

Now how do we pigeonhole the thief? Is he a certain type of human? Surely he could never be corpulent and comfortable, could never be cowardly or nervous. He needs the agility of the tailor, the sinewy muscles of the huntsman and the quick eye of the star-gazer, besides the dexterity of one who has to pocket things. If he is an athlete, he becomes a robber, coarse and cruel; if he is sly, he becomes a swindler; if he is fairly decent, he will be an unreliable rascal. He can make his body thin as a whistle and extricate himself out of any trap. He can change anything, even himself—he is namely a Proteus figure. In another Grimm's tale, "The Master Thief", he is the triumphant actor. In short, as the master of any circumstance, he extracts whatever he pleases from it. The star-gazer turns his eyes to far distances away from the earth but the thief is concerned with earthly matters and the intimacies of others.

Astonishingly enough, tailors are sometimes called in Grimm's tales "thieves" (see "The Tailor in Heaven"), "light-fingered". Tailor and thief are a pair, just as are the huntsman and star-gazer. The tailor cuts things apart, sews pieces together, makes something new out of the stuff. The thief plucks things away, removes, shifts them from one place to another (for instance, one pocket to another). Treasure is

10

changed to a new relationship, whatever the thief himself finds proper. The tailor measures and follows the wishes of the person he is tailoring for. He works at the stuff belonging to another and makes the clothes for him. The thief measures his job using his own wishes and requirements. He fastens on to someone else's possessions for himself, the stuff his eye and desire have fallen upon. His decision is entirely up to him, never mind laws or proper behavior. There have been robbers who held themselves to be heroes and revolutionaries, because they regarded the rich as the true embezzlers. These rebels took it on themselves to bring about equality of wealth, even when it meant breaking the law. One of them is Karl Moor in Schiller's drama *The Robbers*. Another is in the *Hessian Landboten* of the young revolutionary Georg Büchner, whose ideas made the good burghers' hair stand on end; they could well understand the prince, whose gendarmes chased the author all the way to Strassburg because of his "Call to Action". And yet Büchner's "Call" wanted nothing but a fair distribution of wealth. And surely that is what the thief in most cases is aiming for: balancing, equalizing, out of his own free will.

Tailor and thief are the re-formers. If they are bad at their trade, they are really embezzlers. If they are good, they become adjusters. For both, intelligence is the primary factor. Only when they have the clear-sighted talent for joining and uniting (for the tailor, too, must know the tricks of the trade to make his creations sit well) will their handiwork succeed— they also need clever fingers. Both fasten on someone else's possession; the thief makes off with it.

If we look at the huntsman, he too needs a sharp eye and steady hand and should be in no way clumsy. But he uses

11

alert sympathy more than cleverness. In order to be one with nature, he has to love it. He breathes its rhythms in and out, the rhythms of the seasons, of life and death, all the rhythms of natural things and creatures. He makes himself a part of its life, nearby and far off. In giving himself over to the world of nature, the good huntsman becomes its caretaker and nurse. And now the star-gazer: He may not—if he wishes to discover the laws of the stars—interpose himself in the process: he must become a pure mirror of what he sees. Nowhere may his ego-related intelligence take precedence, for he is the objective scientist. He deals in phenomena and lives "furthest out". After reading the stars' ever-changing, ever-moving lives and destinies, he draws their lines of movement. Utmost selfless-ness, devotion to natural laws, are his watchwords.

So we see the unique relationships and contrasts in the four professions. We can even put if like this: the contrasts prove to be transformed similarities. The four different skills of the brothers conceal four different soul activities; we should observe how a special characteristic stands out, heightened, when one particular attitude of soul is unceasingly trained and activated over "four years". Each brother is the master of his craft at the end of that time, just as the tailor was promised, "from the ground up". This really means that the special characteristic of each craft reveals itself in its true per-fection; the four brothers are four soul figures who through their training have reached the perfection of their art, but just because of this perfection, they are one-sided. Each has learned "his" craft, only this and nothing more.

III

After four years the brothers meet again at the crossroads and are united once more. Three of them are carrying a gift from their masters, like a diploma or certificate, though not in writing; it is the tool whose use heightens the proficiency each has reached to an amazing perfection. The tailor is given a needle

"that can sew together whatever comes in your way, whether it is as soft as an eggshell or as hard as steel, and it will join anything so beautifully that no seam will be visible."

The hunter, a gun.

"Whatever you aim at you are sure to hit."

The star-gazer received a telescope with which

"you can discover whatever is going on both in heaven and on earth; nothing can be hidden from you".

The thief, however, received nothing from his master—does he need nothing for his handiwork, or has he everything he needs in himself?

It seems that his capacity and tools are completely one—one whole—a queer idea. Surely he could use, for instance, a magic key? But he himself is a key and this leads us to the conviction that the four brothers represent capacities of the human soul. And how much each has learned! This is evident from the test their father provides, after the happiness of welcoming them home.

" I should like to see what you can do, to prove whether you are as clever as you say." He looked up into the great tree

13

above them and said to his second son, "Among the branches up there near the top there is a chaffinch sitting on her nest; tell me how many eggs are in it." The star-gazer took his glass, looked up and said, "There are five." Then the father said to the eldest, "Go and fetch the eggs down without disturbing the bird who sits brooding on them." The skillful thief climbed up the tree, took the five eggs from under the bird so quietly that she never noticed but remained sitting on her nest quite peacefully, and he brought them down to his father. The father took them, put one of them on each corner of a table and the fifth in the middle, and said to the huntsman. "Can you, with one shot, shoot all five eggs through the middle?" The huntsman aimed and shot the eggs, all five as the father desired, with one shot. He must have had gunpowder for shooting round corners! "Now, it's your turn," said the father to his youngest son. "You shall sew the eggs together again and the young birds inside them as well, and you must do it so that they suffer no injury from the shot." The tailor took his needle and sewed up the eggs as his father wished. When they were finished, the thief had to climb up the tree again and carry them to the nest and lay them under the bird without her being aware of it. The little creature continued to brood over her eggs, and in a few days the young ones crept out of the shells uninjured except that where the tailor had sewn the eggs together, there was a red line around their necks.

In this test the things that happen seem to mock ordinary, natural processes. The invisible is visible to the stargazer, the huntsman shoots around corners, the tailor returns to its living shape what has been totally mangled, and the thief steals the treasure and returns it to its proper place as though nothing had happened inbetween—and the one effect of this magnificent show of talent is the little red collar around the birds' necks; take note: they are chaffinches! Though the whole magic is delightful, from above to below and upwards again, disappearing among the leaves at the top of the tree, we should see it first of all as an example of co-operation, for in this the brothers find their true mastery. And while their father has praise and admiration for each one of them, it is mixed with a bit of worry about their future:

> *'Well, you really can be praised to the skies; you have used your time well and learnt something good. I can't say which of you deserves the most praise. That will be proved if only an opportunity arises to use your talents."*

First of all, we note that the father says, "learnt something good." With that remark our doubt about the thief is relieved. His father recognizes that the eldest son has used his apprenticeship worthily, just as his brothers have done. The eldest is no common pickpocket but "an accomplished thief." His profession, like the others, is indispensable, is even fundamental to the world picture.

The other point that strikes us in the father's speech is his uncertainty about the greatest talent of the brothers: which should earn his highest praise? Although he could not possibly decide, his last sentence holds a new test for his sons; he hints that they should undertake a journey into the world together. With this he is sending them out again into a second apprenticeship, even though they don't realize it. They are already independent persons who can no longer be told, "You must go forth!" but are given simply a hint: "if only an opportunity arises . . . " The father leaves it to them, respecting their freedom.

The brothers seize the suggestion, and now the cheerful prelude leads them to more serious things. A dragon has car-

15

ried off the King's daughter; the King is sorrowing "both by day and by night" and promises her as wife to the one who brings her back. "This would be a fine opportunity for us to show what we can do!" the brothers say to each other. Just as they once set out as boys, leaving their father, they set out together again—but now as masters of their craft. This time they don't come to a crossroads; their independence has been accomplished. This time, too, it is not a separate wandering but a voyage together on a ship, "sailing far over the sea;" one could perhaps call it over the waves of an ocean of spirit.

"I will soon know where she is," said the star-gazer and looked through his telescope. "I can see her already; she is far away from here on a rock in the sea, and the dragon is there too, watching her." Then he went to the King and asked for a ship for himself and his brothers and sailed with them over the sea until they came to the rock. There sat the King's daughter, looking very sad, and the dragon was asleep with his head in her lap. The huntsman said, "I dare not fire, I should kill the beautiful maiden at the same time." "Then I will try my art," said the thief. He climbed up the rock and stole the princess so nimbly that the monster did not move but went on snoring. Full of joy, they hastened away and steered for the ocean.

But the dragon soon awoke and missing the princess, followed them full of rage and came through the air snorting furiously. Just as he hovered over the ship and was ready to pounce down on them, the huntsman shouldered his gun and shot him through the heart. The monster fell down dead but was so large and powerful that his fall shattered the whole ship. Fortunately, however, they contrived to catch hold of a few planks, on which they were able to float on the waves. They were still in great peril, but the tailor took out his wonderful needle and with a few stitches sewed the planks together into a raft. Then they seated themselves

16

upon it and gathered up all the fragments of the ship, even the masts and the sails, and he sewed it all together so that in a very short time the ship was once more seaworthy and they could sail home again in safety.

With extraordinary skill and presence of mind, each brother does what has to be done at the right moment, what no other in his place could do. The four act as one to accomplish their miracle. Without a moment's hesitation, each one knows when his turn has come, from the star-gazer who can establish with his magical vision the "where?" to the thief, to the huntsman and finally to the tailor—the same sequence as before!—so that they finally return home happily with the rescued princess.

"Whosoever brings her back," was the proclamation, "shall be given the princess in marriage." So now on their return, we wonder, puzzled as their father had been on seeing what they could do, for which one was the actual rescuer? "Which of you it is," says the King, "you must settle among yourselves." But this the four brothers cannot do. They begin to quarrel. Each one makes himself important and insists that he alone rescued the princess.

The star-gazer said, "If I had not discovered the princess, all your arts would have been in vain, so she is mine." The thief said, "What would have been the use of your seeing her if I had not got her away from the dragon, so she is mine." The huntsman said, "All of you and the princess would have been torn to pieces by the dragon if my bullet hadn't killed him, so she is mine." The tailor said, "And if I had not sewn the ship together by my art, you would all have been miserably drowned, so she is mine."

Trump and triumph, each one! But the four triumphs actually cancel each other out. Remember: the apprenticeship of the brothers with their master of the crossroads was a time of individual development. Each one became a master of his own craft. When their father sent them into the world again, each thought only of the testing of his own professional art. They didn't notice that their father with hidden wisdom gave them another task: to gain a new, conscious brotherhood. He sent them out to become apprentices of a social order, something much more difficult than the education of individuals. All they had learned separately was put to use marvelously in rescuing the princess; there we have true perfection. But at the last moment the brotherhood seems to fall apart. Thinking back on their adventure, the brothers begin to quarrel before our very eyes, able to speak only "I", "I", "I", "I". They have fallen back to the crossroads of separateness.

The King listens. And to him they owe the testing of their second apprenticeship, for he tells them, "You must decide for yourselves." He is now their master—we can picture it: the King raised on his throne, the brothers quarreling at his feet. What is not clear to them as "facts on firm ground," while they argue, is quite clear to the King looking down on them. Each one is right, each one has given his best and all four were necessary together. And so we hear the King's wise judgment:

"Each of you has an equal right, and as you cannot all have the maiden, none of you shall have her. But I will give each of you as a reward half a kingdom."

The King shows them the truth of the picture as a whole and urges their insight into this, for he wants to prove how limited they must remain as single beings. Even with all their perfection, they are helpless.

The brothers pass the test successfully. The King's decision "pleases them" and they accept it. In other words, each gives

18

up the one-sided kind of superiority he had secretly set his hopes on. With this they raise themselves into the sphere of Kingliness and make themselves capable of carrying a sceptre. "It is better so, than that we should be at variance with each other." The "We" that they discover at this moment springs like a ripe fruit out of the dramatic tension. " They said," the fairy tale puts it, as if the brothers had spoken the "We" out of all four throats at the same time. A circle has rounded, curving itself around the four-part cross of the skills, closing them into one whole.

There are quite a few questions we haven't gone into, chiefly this: why is it that of all the professions in the world, just these four come to the brothers? and how do these professions relate to the age of each brother? and further, what are those extraordinary tools that make the brothers seem even more mysterious?

One thing is certain. None of the four can do a whole job, for it is only when all four work together that they succeed. We can come through this to the insight that the four together are really one, really one whole human being. Even though they appear to us as individuals, the brothers form together a human organism in its fourfold nature. With that in mind, look at the four professions in order to discover how each brother fits himself into the whole and how each one characterizes the four "members" of the human being as described by Rudolf Steiner in *Occult Science*, Chapter II.

The Tailor lives in his own little house and works on his fabrics until they fit the body he is tailoring for. He sits in the chamber of our earthly physical body, visible in the light of day, bringing earth's fabrics into human form. The materials of earth become our bony, mineral structure, which provides the body with firmness. Small and weak as the tailor is, sitting "doubled up in his chamber from morning 'til night" (that is, in bright daylight), driving the needle back and forth, lifting the heavy flatiron, cutting, changing, fitting together whatever material is given him—surely it is the most prosaic of the four crafts, one can even say the most humble. The others look down on him somewhat scornfully; he is always the last. Don't we look at our physical body like this? It seems unspiritual, even coarse to us. The tailor has to do with the body but we should not say that he is the body. He lives in it, is its caretaker. If he stays put within it, he feels like an overburdened servant there, the houseboy or even a slave. It is just this that makes the youngest brother groan as he hears the word "tailor," prompting him to refuse the apprenticeship. But this is the important point: Can there be something more in the ordinary body-tailoring craft that will free it to become an art, "respectable, seemly and very honorable?" Yes, for the Master says, " With me you can learn a very different art of tailoring" and he gives his pupil, as the result of the four years of training, the needle that really can sew together everything, whether delicate as an egg, tender as a bird's throat, hard as steel, or cumbersome as the planks of a ship, sewing it together into something new and whole. We don't find out what takes place during the four years with the mysterious Master, or how the time of these four years is actually measured. The brothers have met with a mystery, each in a different way, but each one changes an ordinary talent into a supernatural ability, judging by their masters' gifts. We see, then, how the tailor, occupying in his ordinary bodily house the most humble place, becomes the one who perfects, completes, consummates and—at the last moment—rescues the work of his brothers. He rescues, we can say, the form, the structure, so that it can become imperishable. For him the phrase fits: the last shall be first. The most wretched handwork can become what lies furthest away: a sublime power to form the spirit. What otherwise might be piecework, the youngest brother can "join together like one piece of stuff" with the help of the wonderful needle. A sliver of steel, this needle, through whose eye the uniting strands of intelligence can be threaded; steel won from purified, hardened iron; iron, the archetype not only of our modern technology but also of the inner texture of our selfhood.

The needle, symbol of uniting, forming, fitting, is the pledge we human beings have to carry back, at the end of our earth-lives, which we spent as householders of our physical body. We, too, are apprentices to a Master from whom we hope some day to receive such a miraculous needle as the certificate that we have completed our learning. Up to now, there has only been One to become a Master, able to transform the body from its decay and death to resurrection. Or has this One already had successors secretly at work on earth—and did one of them take our tailor into his workshop as an apprentice? In his four years the tailor learned the transformation of earthly form, of the bodily nature, into the individual shape that remains firm and strong on the waves of the spirit sea where otherwise all human individuality is apt to drown.

Now, where do we find in ourselves the Huntsman, the early morning forest-wanderer? His domain comprises everything that sprouts and grows; he is friend to every living creature; his heart beats in rhythm with other hearts—of man or animals. He is the rhythmic part of us; we carry him in our body of formative forces, which takes care of our growth, heals our wounds and illnesses, renews our metabolism. We are indebted to him when we wake up refreshed in the morning. He supports the life in us. In our etheric body our "Huntsman" lives and works, he listens to our needs, he brings help to us. Buoyant and resilient, the second brother wanders tirelessly through the etheric realm.

But what is that mysterious gun of his? A good huntsman always uses a good gun, but not necessarily the kind that's quick on the draw. A gamekeeper shoots only when he must, that is, when he finds it essential to root out dangerous or surplus animals. This gun, though, the gift of the Master, shoots around corners. Even when his father sets the eggs askew, off the straight line, the huntsman hits them all with one shot. Look at the exact words: he shoots them all "through the middle;" later on he "shouldered his gun and shot the dragon to the heart." His gun is the huntsman's crown! As apprentice to the unknown Master, he practices devotion to the creatures he takes care of, learns their rhythms, feels their heartbeat. He transforms his instinct into an organ of compassion, one that goes out to all his charges. He would be an unworthy gamekeeper if he failed to love them! That is his real mastery: that he goes directly to the heart when he takes aim. He aims toward the center: from his own heart over to the other heart in one line. We actually find in our huntsman a messenger of the Sun who, taking into his heart the breath of nature, spiritualizes it and sends it out again into the world. His certainty of instinct is transformed into the radiating power of the Sun.

With this the huntsman's ideal work would be the care of a peaceful community of creatures, in fact, Paradise. Warden-preserver would become marksman if danger approached. Facing the enemy, he would focus his Sun-power into a fatal shot. So pure and strong is the heart's lightfilled radiance that when directed outward, it can pierce an evil-doer. Just as the huntsman is able to strike the monster above the ship precisely "to the heart," he can just as precisely radiate healing and affection on those he guards within his own territory. Life and death are placed in the hands of the huntsman; death belongs to life as its counterpart, where he is concerned. As long as we live on earth, looked after by the huntsman, we can breathe peacefully in our earthly body; when he leaves us, we must die. The gun, surely, will be a divine gift to us far in the future and then we will be able consciously to direct the Sun-power of our etheric body. In the meantime the huntsman of our fairy tale has discovered—as Master Marksman—the capacity of the life-spirit. He can command it; we have still to seek it.

What is the enclave of the Star-gazer? He is found at a different layer of our life from his younger brothers, for he works in the realm of our joys and sorrows, our wishes, drives, desires: a secret mobile world that subjects us to a half-conscious, half-unconscious twilight-dream-state. We bear within us a soul-body, interwoven with our physical and etheric bodies, that has been given the name "astral body" by spiritual science. The name reveals its relationship to the stars. Like the planets circling beneath the fixed stars, there move within us courage and clarity, patience and persistence, gaiety and reason, discrimination and compassion. These feelings of ours should circle, but mostly we are satisfied with the mere dark shadows of the genuine forces of feeling, which should be mirror-images of the wandering stars. Thus, we cannot see the stars, as they circle within us—the star-gazer is asleep, covered up in a blanket of dullness. For the star-gazer of our fairy tale, however, the stars in the human soul begin to sparkle; he can behold a starry heaven in himself and discover that it corresponds to the one in the heavens. At the end of his training his Master can give him the all-seeing telescope, the crystal-clear organ of sight/insight; with it, "nothing can be hidden," neither on earth (i.e. in the soul of human beings) nor in heaven (in the spiritual worlds). If only we train ourselves as star-gazers in the selfless observing of the weaving, circling planetary influences, we will be at home, both here in our body and there in the stars. Our star-gazer transforms his art of seeing into an awakened soul-power that can itself become spirit. And so the "skillful" star-gazer with his contemplative wisdom is the first one to know (as purest kind of scientist) where the starting points for new initiatives can be striven for and discovered. Before the father speaks to his oldest son, the thief, he speaks first to the star-gazer. Before the thief is called on to contribute his special skill, the star-gazer has to reveal the goal, the "where?" that has to come before the "how?".

The most important element of the human entity is the Self, the independent ego, the part of us that makes us truly human. Our physical body we have in common with minerals, the etheric body with the plants, the astral body with the animal kingdom (for they, too, experience pain and joy)—but the ego is our very own possession. Every person has his own ego; no one can take away what once it has acquired. Anything and everything can disappear into it without leaving a trace. The ego can appropriate, in a soul-spiritual sense, whatever comes near its grasp, for with it we develop our thinking, our concepts, whereby we make every perception our own property. The ego is the apprehender, the "thief" in us. By means of the ego the Self becomes a lordly sovereign, a spirit among spirits. Memories and recollections are collected by the ego and stored up; everything that we have ever taken hold of is freed from time and space; the ego lets us belong to every epoch, every part of the world. The strongest lock can not separate the ego away from what has happened or is happening. With every perception we steal something from the world outside us to add to our store of treasure, "so cleverly that others will never find it out." Everything goes on as before, but now we "have it."

We should remember that our thief received no special gift from his Master. His own nature is the key he uses to take possession of things. We carry this apprehending key well developed within us, but whether it always seeks worthwhile treasure is another question. The nature of the thief certainly coincides with his key because of his "age". He is the oldest of the four brothers: this means, the highest in rank. Through the gift of the ego, the human being carries a spiritual commission from the gods. The original ego-substance, gift of the highest spiritual entities, is divine. We are "the sons of God", the *New Testament* tells us. The other constituents of the human being are also children of cosmic powers; our fairy tale simplifies this fact rather sweepingly when it describes the brothers as sons of *one* father, appearing in different epochs of development. Our physical body in its mineral form was crystallized out as the last component: the tailor is the youngest son. He appears as visible, material body on the mineral earth and will reach his spiritual goal as the last of the four.

We carry around in us the four brothers; however, they are different from those in the tale. We unite in ourselves the ordinary, natural four, but in the fairy tale we meet the *skillful* brothers! The title of the story points us toward the future, for it means that our natural, inborn abilities must be changed into greater ones. The fairy tale figures are images of the mysterious, still hidden parts of ourselves that will some day be the transformations of our ordinary qualities; in short, they are the highest ideals for our future, these four: Thief, Stargazer, Huntsman, Tailor. We are to become like them and for this the Masters give us four long cosmic years' time. The end of the transforming process will come only when the youngest brother, the Tailor, has become a Master and can govern his needle. But truly, his art is not the most humble of the four!

At the end of the fairy tale, all the brothers become kings. What does it mean, to rescue the princess from the dragon? — Surely, to free the soul in its innate beauty from world-darkness. A double-kingdom ("I will give to each of you, as a reward, half a kingdom") can then be founded; heaven and earth are brought together. Tailor and Huntsman, representing our earthly nature (physical-etheric), unite with Stargazer and Thief, our cosmic-heavenly parts (soul and spirit). We belong to both heaven and earth, and at the end of the tale, two brothers share each of the kingdoms. However, they are all four united in the human being himself, united with each other, and at the end, finally, united with their father. In the double-kingdom of his sons, the father now shares in the wealth that long beforehand he divined in his wisdom as slumbering within them. His trust has borne fruit; his sons have passed the tests of self-formation and brotherhood.

Brotherhood and self-formation are related as circle and cross. The end of the tale provides a strangely similar image to the beginning, from its start in the sheltered home belonging to the father—the circle—to the dynamics of being sent off and separating at the crossroads. As masters, so much later, they meet again at the crossroads and raise the cross of their individual skills, resolute, all four of them, omnipotent but separate and self-concerned. Only at the moment that brings them to the "We together" can they bring about the circle again. Then, in the unending wholeness of the circle, each can remain himself: *a cross within the circle.* It is the meaning of mankind's slow development that the symbols, divided in the past, should find their way together and become integrated. We can perceive in this the birth of a union of earth and heaven, a double-kingdom, in human beings. Earlier the Christ aura of sun circle and cross was described. We can try to understand the skills of the brothers as the effect of the Christ event on mankind, a cosmic-earthly event. At the end of the fairy tale come the words, "And they lived with their father in the greatest happiness." Simply and humanly put, in fairy tale style, it is a paraphrase of Christ's saying: I and the Father are one. The path is long; it is the path of transformation that leads toward fulfillment.

For further reading:

Rudolf Steiner, *The Poetry and Meaning of Fairy Tales,*
Mercury Press, 1990.

Rudolf Meyer, *The Wisdom of Fairy Tales,* Anthroposophic
Press, 1989.

Rudolf Geiger, *About "The Sea Hare",* Mercury Press, 1990.